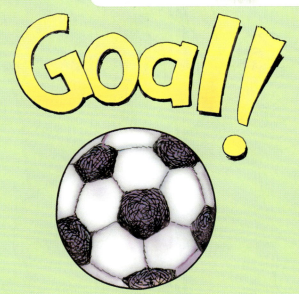

Goal!

by Rory Thomas
illustrated by
Sheila Bailey

MODERN CURRICULUM PRESS
Pearson Learning Group

"Can you help me?" said Kit.

"I can get it," said Tim.

"Can you help me?" said Kit.

"I can get it," said Tim.

"Can you help me?"
said Kit.

"I can get it," said Tim.

"I can not get it!" said Tim.
"I can get it," said Kit.
Goal!